M000209161

Field Notes

Field Notes

Poems by Margaret Rogal

Illustrations by Mike Jacobs

A Little Book about North Dakota, Volume I

NDSU | NORTH DAKOTA STATE UNIVERSITY PRESS

Fargo, North Dakota

NDSU NORTH DAKOTA STATE
UNIVERSITY PRESS

Dept. 2360, P.O. Box 6050, Fargo, ND 58108-6050
www.ndsupress.org

Field Notes
Poetry by Margaret Rogal

Copyright © 2022 North Dakota State University Press
First Edition
First Printing
A Little Book about North Dakota Series, Volume 1

ISBN: 978-1-946163-49-3
LCCN: 2021949484

Cover design by Jamie Trosen
Interior design by Deb Tanner

Director: David Bertolini
Publisher: Suzzanne Kelley
Series Editor: Mike Jacobs
Editorial Administrative Assistant: Sarah W. Beck
Assistant Acquisitions Editor: Kyle Vanderburg
Graduate Assistant in Publishing: Oliver M. Sime
Editorial Intern: Megan G. Brown

The publication of *Field Notes* is made possible by The Muriel and Joseph Richardson Fund and the generous support of donors to the NDSU Press Fund and the NDSU Press Endowment Fund.

For copyright permissions, please contact Suzzanne Kelley at 701-231-6848 or suzzanne.kelley@ndsu.edu.

Printed in the United States of America

I am afraid that, at first, the memory of old Connecticut hills in blossom time was too strong and I could not imagine how grass and flowers could spring from the heavy black mud, and without flowers how could there ever be any birds.

—Robert Silliman Judd, Cando, North Dakota, April 1909

Contents

Foreword

There is a direct link between the poems in *Field Notes* and the pioneer birdmen of North Dakota: the poet Margaret Rogal. She is the granddaughter of Robert Silliman Judd, who was the nephew of Elmer Judd, which makes Rogal the great-grandniece of the most esteemed birdman that North Dakota has ever known, perhaps excepting John James Audubon.

Elmer Taylor Judd was not himself a North Dakota product. He grew up in Connecticut. Likewise, his nephew Robert Silliman Judd was born in Connecticut and spent most of his life there except for a notable six months with Uncle Elmer in North Dakota.

Both of these Judds knew their birds, and Elmer knew North Dakota. When he was twenty-one years old, in 1887, Elmer homesteaded in Dakota Territory, two years before North Dakota became a state. His homestead was near Cando in Towner County. This location was a fortunate choice, as Towner County lies astride the Central Flyway. In Judd's time, as now, tremendous numbers of waterfowl pass through Towner County. Judd, however, was hardly satisfied with the ducks and geese; he became familiar with the wide range of prairie birds, from the conspicuous waterfowl, through the shorebirds, all the way to the prairie passerines, including the sparrows. In 1917, he published the names of 250 species he had encountered in a book called *A List of North Dakota Birds Found in the Big Coulee, Turtle Mountains and Devils Lake Region*.

Judd's reputation as a crackerjack birdman attracted the preeminent birders of his time to North Dakota. He met them all and showed them all the birds he had found, but his interest was not limited to seeing and identifying birds. He served as North Dakota's game and fish commissioner for several years in the early 1920s.

Soon after he died in 1941, *The Wilson Bulletin*—now called *The Wilson Journal of Ornithology*—printed an essay appreciative of Judd's life work. Its author was O. A. Stevens, who spent his career studying North Dakota's plant life. In the essay, Stevens describes a field trip with Judd and several other birdmen. Among them was L. B. Bishop, a medical doctor from New Haven, Connecticut, and a noted amateur ornithologist and collector, who made four trips to North Dakota in 1895, 1901, 1902, and 1905.

Robert Silliman Judd, Elmer's nephew, ventured west from Connecticut to North Dakota in 1909 when he was twenty-two. He spent six months in the state, from April to November. After long days of helping Elmer on the farm, Robert roamed the surrounding prairie collecting specimens, many of them for Yale University, where they still reside. The Silliman name is significant in Yale University history. Benjamin Silliman, an ancestor, had helped establish Yale's medical school.

Enter Margaret Rogal. A librarian by profession, she knew of her grandfather's interest in birds, but she was unprepared for the trove she found when she took possession of her grandfather's archives. The archival documents include lists and descriptions of birds he had seen and collected in North Dakota, as well as letters home describing the landscape and family farm. This serendipity inspired the poems presented here, which describe the birds that Robert Judd encountered; his family, including his beloved aunt Susie and three lively young cousins; and the mysterious beauty that the rugged prairie slowly revealed to him.

Of course, there is a kind of tension between the collecting techniques employed by Elmer Judd and his nephew, and the techniques used today to identify birds. In the early twentieth century, birders shot the bird, skinned it, and shipped it to collectors in the East. In her poem "Ruby-crowned Kinglet," Rogal highlights this tension, but the issue threads itself through many of the poems. Rogal struggles with Robert's hunting, but in the midst of questioning his practice, she understands its context and, as well, Robert's love of the creatures he kills.

The Judds were splitters, eager to find new species or to describe new subspecies. Many of today's students of birds hesitate at the finely drawn distinctions that the Judds and others drew. Without doubt, they were keen observers. Bishop named a subspecies of Song Sparrow after Judd, *Melospiza fasciata juddi,* the Dakota Song Sparrow. Bishop thought its plumage and especially its voice distinguished it from other song sparrows. Alas for the bird's namesake, the lumpers have prevailed and combined the subspecies with *Melospiza melodia.* There is a poem here that describes this bird and the panoply of sparrows that fill the bird books.

In these wry and whimsical poems, from a rhyming sonnet about the vulnerability of prairie ground nests in "Nest," to a riff on the alphabet poem in "An Alphabet of Yellowlegs," to an exploration of the visual representations of Flycatchers' songs in "Song Drawings," to a prose poem that captures the droll habits and spectacular plumage of the "Green-winged Teal," as well as the cavalier hunters who take her down, Margaret Rogal reinforces and enlarges the legacy of the Judd family, adding her uniquely important contribution to our knowledge and appreciation of North Dakota's birds.

Mike Jacobs, Series Editor
A Little Book about North Dakota

Author's Note

Based on my grandfather Robert Silliman Judd's field notebooks, letters, and memoir, these poems describe Robert's experience as a twenty-two-year-old New Englander visiting his uncle Elmer Judd's farm in Cando, North Dakota, from April to November 1909. The poems reflect Robert's burgeoning participation in and understanding of family and farm life, but—most importantly—his profoundly expanding knowledge of and love for birds of the prairie. Excerpts from Robert's writings alternate with the poems.

Unless otherwise noted, the names of species of birds are the ones Robert used in 1909.

Letter to Pop
April 19, 1909

Monday morning we hitched up old Bronc and another horse which he keeps here in Cando and drove out to the farm. It is eight miles north across a rolling prairie country. The land immediately around Cando is about as flat as a ballroom floor but as you go north it becomes more rolling and there are frequent potholes, sloughs and coulees, and right here I may as well tell what these terms signify.

Flat as a Ballroom Floor

that's what it's like here
all around Cando

field and stubble
brown and yellow
shimmering loam, glancing gloom, bits of crimson heather

there are roads if you like
but Uncle Elmer drives across every pothole, coulee, and slough
Old Bronc patient as a sunflower

only it's not a breeze, it's a wind
that pounds your head, makes it fairly ache

until the sun comes out
until you can read in the house until nearly eight o'clock

mallards and pintails by the hundreds
Snow Geese by the thousands
every little body of water

every dip and rise

Uncle Elmer has never seen so much game
it would be a hard matter to shoot them
as they are quite wild

white like a snowbank, the occasional blue
slough
Aunt Sue

after dark
the geese fly over the house
I hear them talking
each kind of goose has a peculiar honk of its own

a wind-gray, night-blue song

thank you for the long letter, Mother, Pop, Irene

Summary of visit

Shot my first specimens, 3 male Lapland
Longspurs. They are very common everywhere as
are also Horned Larks and Snowflakes although
the Longspurs are by far the most numerous. These
birds congregate in huge flocks of thousands and
scatter across the fields feeding together. Often it
seemed as tho every bird in one of the flocks was
singing.

Lapland Longspur

Naturalists Describing the Lapland Longspur
Calcarius lapponicus

1. Voice

Amongst a flock of Larks or Buntings, the Lapland Longspur's
dry rattle can be detected immediately followed by *ticky-tick-teu.*

Flight song sweet and bubbling,
a gentle, jingling warble *freew didi freer di fridi fideew*
with rich husky quality.

Common call a rough whistled *tleew,*
in summer a sharp whistled *chich* and *chi-kewoo.*

2. Habitat

Winters in open windswept fields
and on grassy coastal dunes.

(Fields must be windswept.
Dunes must be grassy).

3. Identification

Like Snow Buntings and Horned Larks, they often *run*
(but occasionally take big hops, so, when you see them,
they may be in their hopping phase).

Some black streakings
varying amount of reddish
often a smudge of streaks.

But the wings are definite. The wings show much less white than other Longspurs.

And, in the spring, both sexes acquire a black throat.
Otherwise, the female is much more beautiful.

4. Migration

The Lapland Longspur is the only Longspur that is common east of the plains.
Winters regularly in New York. Not Vermont. But it flies through
on its way to parking lots along the coast.

If you are lucky, if you are good, in a barren field in November
a whole flock will dart into the air.

Summary of visit

The next day . . . I recorded Juncos, Red-winged
Blackbird, Blue Geese, Am. White-footed Geese,
Hutchins Geese, Snowy Owl and Prairie Chicken,
and this list might be considered the vanguard of
the Spring migration.

Dark-eyed Junco

Sibley, 2014: *Junco hyemalis*

Junco hyemalis: reed of the winter. A bird like a reed
because it was first spotted among reeds,
which are propagated by rhizomes, like iris.
Iris bird.
Snow bird.

Family: emberizine. Of the ember-birds: small, glowing, fiery.
I don't think the junco is often secretive.
Rather: pert, chatty, funny-flash.
Not afraid of my shadow-walk,
confident it can fly into the nearest bush.
Dooryard bird.

Maybe oboe-bird, tiptoe, hello-bird.
Maybe yellow-sorrow, or long ago, or to-and-fro.

Nest is a cup. In a meadow. A small hollow
scratched in old grass, as round as a banjo,
as musical, as pure-and-simple.
Slate-and-white,
cameo, clover roll.

Sometimes, this-or-that:
smack stip
tzeet
tinkle chip
keew
tsititit tit

Summary of visit

Saw a flock of hundreds of Snow Geese settle onto a stubble field. Drove up back of a rise and as we got where we could see over, the whole flock was bunched together on the ground. They made a great white bank like snow. When they flew we could see a few Blue Geese among them.

Snow Goose

Snow Goose

Judd, 1909: *Chen hypeborea*
Peterson, 1939: *Chen hyperborea*
Sibley, 2014: *Chen caerulescens*

Of the far north, of the Arctic tundra, where the Snow Goose nests.
Of blue essence, because snow has a blue tinge in its coldest shadows.
Or because the Snow Goose can be Blue.

A dark goose in a flock of Snows is probably a Blue.
Blue's voice: exactly like a Snow's.
Both have pink bills and legs.

Then there is the Greater and the Lesser.
Couldn't they be the Larger and the Smaller, or
the Longer and Shorter, or Fran and Jim,

Jimmie being my mother's name?
The softness of snow, the goofiness of geese.
They mate for life. Why would you shoot one?

Letter to Pop
April 19, 1909

Wednesday afternoon we hitched the horses to his spring wagon and drove for three hours across the prairie looking for some stray horses. Driving out here isn't like driving at home. Of course there are roads if you like, but when Uncle Elmer drives he goes across plowed fields, stubble, coulees, or anything else that happens to be in the way.

Uncle Elmer

Helter-skelter Uncle Elmer, helmsman, as if the prairie
were a sea, crest and trough, hill and dale.

No matter about roads: he drives across plowed fields,
stubble, coulees, or anything else that happens to be in the way.

Just like the dog Fritz, "the cheerful idiot," who splashes into
every mudhole, and usually has a gopher in his mouth.

On mirage mornings, you can see as far as Perth
and beyond.

Uncle Elmer says we'll bring our blankets and camp
at the farm this summer: perfect pal.

I had the laugh on Uncle Elmer: one day last week
his driving team turned the buggy over and broke the pole.

Uncle Elmer says it would be better if you would ship us
a barrel of those early apples instead of telling us about them.

Letter to Pop
April 19, 1909

So much for the livestock now as to his help. He has
a family of Danes on the farm. A man and wife, one
son about eighteen and a girl about twelve besides two
small boys. He pays the man and wife forty a month
besides their board and the boy thirty besides. But
he thinks they will be worth it. The man has been a
farmer in Minnesota and is especially good with
horses and cattle. The woman is big and strong, a good
cook and willing. Uncle Elmer says he guesses it will
be up to him to furnish the grub and she will keep us
in good shape. He tells Aunt Susie he is taken better
care of out to the farm than he is at home.

Aunt Susie

The Dane and Aunt Susie, two women taking care of boys. What happens
when Aunt Susie goes to the farm? Do they talk? Does Aunt Susie say,
Hello, Dagmar, Gertrud, or Marta? Maybe they have tea, and are grateful
to share the cooking, laundry, cleaning, and worrying, the mud and blood.

Maybe you don't notice because you're in the field running the binder
and scrutinizing birds. Maybe Aunt Susie's kitchen smells good when she's
frying chicken, although you like duck a bit better, maybe much better.
Too many chickens, too scrawny, too wild. Feathers. Skin. Bones. Wishbone.

Three galloping, climbing, jumping boys scare Aunt Susie, each intent
on copying what the others do, better, faster, riskier. Aunt Susie who makes
strawberry shortcake every week, who walks to the neighbors' to procure
tea leaves for your stye, who sits up at night coughing, who laughs and frets,

who would like to cook for your pop, to see him out here on the farm.
You hate to leave; she makes the prairie feel like home. You'll miss her.
You will not see her again once you board the train for Mother and Pop.
In time for Thanksgiving. Who will cough to death.

Skins
May 11, 1909

152. American Pipit
Anthus pensilvanicus
Le. 6.75   Ex 10.75
Shot near slough. single bird

Summary of visit

I was told on good authority that a very faint
song apparently way up in the blue was made by a
Sprague's Pipit and that if I had patience to wait
and watch for an hour or two it might condescend to
come to earth and then if I proved extremely quick
and sharp of eye I might catch a glimpse before he
gained cover.

American Pipit

Anthus pensilvanicus

single bird
no period even
but a pause   a breath
as if paying respects
there was only one

impossible
to see the flock
walk briskly in all directions
bob their tails
was it thirsty   dusty

American
pipits might breed on
bogs and marshes   although
my mother didn't
speak of them

secretive
especially the Sprague's
which is not found
here   if only you
waited for the Sprague's

Pipit   if I
have the patience
I might note the Pipit too
way up in the blue
plummet to earth

Skins
May 19, 1909

181.   Ruby-Crowned Kinglet
       Regulus calendula
       Le. 4.25 Ex. 6.50
       Shot while feeding in willow bush on prairie.

Ruby-crowned Kinglet

Ruby-crowned Kinglet
Regulus calendula

You started shooting birds when you were fifteen.
You were twenty-two when you shot 181,
a Ruby-crowned Kinglet,
her name longer than her body.

Couldn't you have left that number out?
The one thin, diminutive, like the bird herself,
feeding on a willow branch,
ruffling her leaf-wings, her leaf-heart.

She isn't crowned red,
leaving that to the male because he is the defender,
the little king,
who hovers near when she's building the nest,
when she's brooding,
when she hurries to build a second nest,
so many eggs, so many young,
so many possible deaths of children.

I suppose that is why we know about her white eye ring,
because you shot her,
held her in your hand, examined, listed, classified, and skinned her,
her olive cape,
which you donated to Dr. Bishop, for proof.

You noticed how beautiful she was,
although you didn't record that thought in your notes or letters,
writing to your mother a few days later,
The boys just brought in a big bunch of dandelion blossoms,
the first of the season.
With love to yourself and the rest.
Robert

Skins
May 19, 1909

182.   Black Tern
       Hydrochelidon nigra surinamensis
       Male
       Le. 10.25 Ex. 24.50
       Killed with horse whip by man riding gang plow.

Black Tern
Hydrochelidon nigra surinamensis

At some point, one must know the difference between a gull
and a tern.

I'm sure I've seen terns on the beaches of Long Island Sound,
but their gull-likeness, their sea-birdness,
their formations sweeping over the water like arrows.

Their slender build, forked tails, bills pointed down towards the water,
their grace.

Ah, Emily said, I perceive the rose!
Did Emily know the tern?

The Black Tern's head is black when breeding, whitish with smudges of black
when not breeding.
They do not normally swim; gulls do.

Maybe I can discern the Black Tern. But I can't discern the:

> Least
> Royal
> Elegant
> Sandwich
> Roseate

Perhaps the Black Tern appears in northern Vermont.

Perhaps the man riding the plow killed a Black Tern by accident,
snapping his whip over the horse's back.

Perhaps he felt great sorrow, retrieved the bird, delivered it to my grandfather,
who observed its black head, gray wings, long bill,
who skinned it carefully.

Skins
May 20, 1909

185. Bobolink
      Dolichonyx oryzivorus
      (male) Le. 7.60 Ex. 12
      One of flock on wire fence

Bobolink

Dolichonyx oryzivorus

> "'Lethe' in my flower,
>   of which they who drink,
>   in the fadeless Orchards
>   hear the bobolink!"
>   —Emily Dickinson, #54

You say the bird is common—
the Bob O'Lincoln—Bobolink—
but I've never seen one
tilting on a leaf. *Pink, pink,*

he pipes, his crisp black trousers—
his clean white shirt—
as if dressed for a ball, or
to meet the president!

Winking this way and that—
his gurgle, bubble, trill—
not much bigger
than a sunflower's frill.

But Emily says, listen!
Emily says, look!
Emily says, drink
in my own, my brook.

See not just the petal—
not just the flake—
not just Jupiter—
(a faraway lake!)—

but an orchard all alight—
an apple's bloom—
a bird in black and white
waving on a stem.

You took a skin, just one—
not to bother—
not to mention—his home
a pretty meadow.

You missed him, skipped
Him—magician—king—
as he sheds his silver suit
for a morning dress, a wing

tawny and streaked—
velvet like a rose—
like a field in fact
decked out in yellow clothes—

so don't neglect the common
the soft and overlooked—
bobbin bird, linchpin—
fearless anchor Bobolink!

Field Notes
May 27, 1909

8. Chestnut-collared Longspur

Nest set 2" below level of ground on gravelly prairie hill. Made of fine grasses and a few tufts of cowhair.

Sat down to pick a few yellow violets when the female came running around in front of me. Sat perfectly still and she soon worked back to her nest which was about five feet in back of me.

Yellow Violets

I sat down on a gravelly hillock
to pick yellow violets

when a Chestnut-collared Longspur
hopped round in front of me

she wasn't bothered wasn't flustered
I stayed as still as possible

and on her cheek a yellow blush
as if a violet's brush

had deposited there its dust
a telltale sign of stepping among the violets

my tiny bouquet an offering
to the bird's tiny nestlings

barely five feet in back of me
who would have guessed?

Field Notes
June 2, 1909

10. Pintail
*Nest a hollow in clump of grass in low field near a
slough and coulee. Was walking through grass when
she flew from almost under my feet. Merely flew out
of the nest and plopped along over the grass for fifty
feet. Then walked around where she could keep her
eye on me. Seven fresh eggs. She left nest so collected
them June 9.*

Pintail

Dafila acuta

She flew!
From under your feet
as you walked in a field,

with a rush of wings,
of feathers!
Her brown buffy mottled feathers,

her gray bill,
her gray eye watching you,
she knew your tricks.

The old bird left the nest;
you collected her eggs,
seven fresh pale-olive eggs,

from her nest in a hollow.
Where was the male?
Dabbling in the slough?

His elegant black and white suit,
his long pointed tail—
flagpole, baton, needle.

Imperious prince, where was he?
White streak up his long neck,
his field mark, his character,

drawn in soft grays and white,
labeled "PINTAIL"
as if the artist,

the bird watcher,
knew better than to whistle,
clap, or cry out.

Field Notes
June 2, 1909

11. Chestnut-collared Longspur
Nest in hollow scratched in grass in low level
meadow between wheat fields. Made of grass lined
with very fine grass and set so that edge was even
with ground. Flushed female.

Nest

> "To touch [the nest] is to be as close to its maker
> as to touch a brush stroke of a Van Gogh sunflower."
> —Mike Hansell, Professor Emeritus, University of Glasgow

Hollowed in a field, can you call this dent a nest,
this shallow in the stubble, this teacup in the grass?
Hidden, she hopes, from blade, boot, and crest,
her house a mere dimple, a dip, a bend of thatch.

She had no appointment, not with you, not a tryst.
She's doing nothing but bathing in the dust
as the sun lines the prairie, orange, in the east,
as thin, as faint, as blood running in your wrist,

or is it evening now, do you hear vespers voices,
crickets, birdlings, a mouse's tiny whispers?
With only a claw, only a beak, without any fuss,
she scratched her homely cradle in the brush.

But wait, you approach! You stamp, bark, and kick!
Flushed, she looks back at you, her bird-heart crushed!

14.   Canvas-back

Nest in large patch of reeds near center of big
slough. The tops had been broken down and drawn
together and other reeds woven in so as to make a big
platform the size of a bushel basket. The top of nest
was a foot above the water. Nest a hollow in this mass
lined with down. Found on May 24 with nine eggs
but did not or could not tell what they were. Today
flushed bird and shot her. Nine eggs. inc. ½

Canvasback

Aythya vallisneria

When Dr. Bishop noticed this empty dry quiver, this weathered wallet,
this pale reddish head sloping to a long black bill, her brown eye forever
shocked, forever stung by the boom and burn, the failure to lift, dive, and nibble,
to count her gray-green eggs, he stored her in his backyard shed, gave her
later to Chicago. She traveled like you did, by train, back and forth across
the country, landing in the middle, her short down-turned tail, her quack,
her bushel-basket nest slung over the slough, her conviviality, making a ruckus,
making a V.

Canvasback:
because her back is strong
because she sheds water
because she's woven like a khaki rucksack—
windblown cattail—saltmarsh rowboat—pitpat wingbeat—gunshot.

Field Notes
June 4, 1909

Wilson's Phalarope nest roughly made of grass. Placed in slight hollow in short green grass near a grassy slough. Flushed male from nest. He chased up female and then I collected the pair. Four eggs, fresh.

Wilson's Phalarope

Steganopus tricolor

A short poem for a small bird although her legs are long
and straw-colored, her bill long and needle-like;
on water she spins like a top while dabbling
for tiny aquatic animals, dizzy silly show.
Getting fat, she can hardly fly,
her black eye-stripe blending into cinnamon,
her pearl-gray head, her bright white breast
irresistible to the male who takes care, finally,
keeping watch as you, hunter, you, thief, raid the nest
of its four spotted eggs, then "take" the birds,
their scolding not deterring you, you admirer of Wilson's Phalarope
(meaning *fringe-foot*)
Spin—dab—spin—dab—spin—dab—*quoit—quoit—quoit—*
their frog-like murmur.

Field Notes
June 11, 1909

27.   *Yellow-headed Blackbird*
Nest woven to bunch of dead cattails in patch of
cattails in grassy slough. Made of strips torn from the
leaves of cattails, the fine and smoother pieces being
on the inside. Very compact and strongly made and
woven to the stems about 2 ft. above the water. 4 eggs.
inc. 1/3

Yellow-headed Blackbird

Yellow-headed Blackbird

Xanthocephalus xanthocephalus

Someday I will go to the Yale Peabody Museum of Natural History
and ask to see the Yellow-headed Blackbird collected by R. S. Judd
in 1909. I was there as a kid, but no one mentioned, did they, that my
grandfather's bird specimens lay in a drawer downstairs. Did he visit
his specimens? How did he transport all those skins from North Dakota
to Connecticut? He must have shipped them, packing them carefully
in the pages of *The Cando Herald*. I could have seen a Yellow-headed
Blackbird in the wild when I lived in Iowa, but at that time I wasn't
lonely and I wasn't bird-conscious. I was eager. I wasn't thinking of
my grandfather, shooting birds just a bit northwest. The female is duller,
the guide says. But that wording was changed, because she's like heather
or a fall leaf. Autumn leaf. The girl whose name is Autumn. Of course,
he fell in love with her. Not my grandfather. He fell in love with Edith,
of riches, of war. Edith wasn't rich or warlike. Did my grandfather show
Edith his specimens? Did he take her to the museum to capture his past,
to show her his warlike side, although he loved the nests, how they were
tied to cattails above the water, how the finer round grasses lined the nest,
how the bird could discern this, the difference between coarser and finer,
rougher and smoother, flat and round. Luxury. Comfort. Watertight.
Hanging there over the slough, this basket nest of the Yellow-headed
Blackbird. Males tend the young along with the females, although usually
only the first brood. After that, he's too busy defending his females from
Marsh Wrens and Striped Skunks and other Yellow-headed Blackbirds,
just like him.

Letter to Pop
June 14, 1909

Have one set of Killdeer found by the man at the farm, they are very common but one of the hardest nests to find. As soon as you step into a field there will be two or three of them following you around and calling "killdee" in the most heartbreaking tone you ever heard, as if they had nests all over the farm.

Killdeer

Oxyechus vociferus

When the man on the farm, the man who plows, feeds the animals
and curries them, births lambs and shears sheep, who has four children,
whose wife takes good care of you, better than Aunt Susie, when
that man finds the Killdeer's nest, he collects the eggs, four pale buff
eggs with blackish brown spots—and gives them to you.

How did the man stop his horse, and not plow under the nest?
Was it the Killdeer's agitation, her dragging her wing as if wounded,
her crying and squawking, flapping and skittering, flying into his face,
as if wanting to wound him, too? She only succeeded in drawing him
ever closer to her nest on the bare ground.

You shot five Killdeers for their skins—two black breast bands,
golden-red rumps and tail feathers, broad wingstripe—not for their voice,
which you couldn't capture, collect, or skin. You paused in your day-long
round of the pasture, your heart breaking five times over, as the bird rose
on the wind, calling *kill-dee, kill-dee*. Also, *dee-dee-dee*.

Field Notes
June 18, 1909

38. Shoveller
Nest set deep down in bunch of fine praire grass near center of piece of dry level praire between fields. 12 eggs nearly ready to hatch. Nest heavily lined with down. Saw her on the nest although the grass was drawn over in such a way that only part of her back was visible. I stood directly over her and kicked the grass twice before she would leave. She then flew off feigning broken wings etc. after the usual manner of all ducks.

Shoveller

Peterson, 1939: *Spatula clypeata*

There are those soft drawings again in shades of white gray and black
the Shovellers
flying with the Blue-winged Teal   Green-winged Teal   and Baldpate

dark   white   dark   white   dark
that is the pattern of the Shoveller

and there she is   swimming
her *tremendous long and flattened bill*
whether spoon-shaped   shovel-shaped   or spatulate
combing the water for *minute aquatic animals*

you say she is the least suspicious duck
her blue wing patches   her spoon bill
the broad pale edges of her wings

no longer   you scared her   her young
you killed two
did you eat them
you say you like duck rather better than chicken

after you stamped in the grass
after you collected the eggs
after you tied the horses and shot the Shovellers

she is now the most suspicious duck
her light quack becoming a squawk
becoming beating wings
becoming broken.

Field Notes
June 18, 1909

36. Sora

Nest cleverly woven of dead grass placed in a bunch of all green grass, the top being drawn in so as to form a sort of dome about 8" above the nest, the whole forming a very pretty green bower. When first found the water stood all around the nest over 6" deep but now it is quite dry. 12 eggs Did not see bird at all.

Sora

Porzana carolina

It's not fall and you didn't toss a stone into the marsh
so of course you didn't hear the Sora cry, "Keek!"

instead far away in the farmhouse
you heard its weird laughing night-sound

this small round fluff of a bird with a bright yellow stubby bill
jumping about on its long-toed feet

busy shy watchful nervous
but happy oh so happy cheerful that's why it laughs at night

and lays a great many eggs cinnamon-buff
with dark brown spots

how green its nest an arched dome
a pretty green bower and if the nest is full the Sora simply

lays a few eggs in the neighbor's nest
woven shyly woven tightly above the marsh

Porzana
a Venetian term that means "small rail"

how exotic a name as if I called my child *Piccola*
because I liked the way it sounded

when you saw the bird at the edge of the grassy slough
you took a picture

then you shot her just like that
there are some puzzles that remain so.

Letter to Mother
June 20, 1909

*Now mother I hope you won't go and show my
letters to everybody. I like to write to you alone.
They can read pop's if they like.*

Dear Mother, My Dear Mother, Dearest Mother,

I wish I could
see some roses,
could see them
in blossom,
know which ones
came through the winter.
Did my ramblers amount to anything this year?
I like to know
just which ones
came through.

I wish someone would write and tell me
how these things are going.

You won't show my letters to anyone
will you, Mother?
I like to write to you alone.

Which ones came through?
Will I come through?

The wind makes my head ache
as if the mosquitoes would eat me alive
all day long.

I planted a flower garden for Aunt Susie.
She says she wants to cook
a dinner for you once.
She says don't mention scallops again
unless you can ask her to dinner.

Carrots out here,
they make good pie
and fine sweet pickles as good as pears.

I wish I could
have some
of that strawberry shortcake.
I wish someone would write.

I told Aunt Susie
that it would seem almost like leaving home,
I have been here so long now.

The boys say I must stay
and eat turkey with them
but I tell them
I am going to be
with my ma and pa
on that day anyway.

So goodbye for now,
my own dear
mother and father.

Your loving son,
Robert.

Letter to Mother
June 29, 1909

Then Aunt Susie is not at all well, has a bad cough which often keeps her awake all night, besides she worrys and frets a good deal about different things. She has been very good to me and I know would hate to have me go but still I know I am quite a little extra trouble to her. She has just now come in from the neighbors with some tea leaves for my eye.

Calling Card: "Mrs. Elmer T. Judd"

I wonder if you, Susan Curtis Booth, had your calling card
printed in Bridgeport at the time of your marriage to Elmer T. Judd,
before you left for Cando, North Dakota, before you knew
what you were in for: train chugging over muddy prairie, thin

town, scant houses, curve of the earth seeming to flatten out
on mirage mornings. No visits, no leaving your card in a basket
on a porch, only a long walk to the closest neighbor to borrow tea
for a poultice. Are your collars, neck ribbons, and brooches laid

away in a trunk at the foot of your bed? You saved one card,
the curly black letters printed on white laid paper, or wove, or linen,
or look-alike, *Mrs. Elmer T. Judd*, neat as a pin, sweet as a posy,
like a bit of lace, like a frill. A sign of what you gave up to become

Mrs. Elmer T. Judd, a memory of stateliness, of life in Bridgeport,
where you plan to return when you die, dressed finely.

Summary of visit

A very common bird on the prairie and perhaps too you will think a very ordinary one but of which I became very fond is the Western Meadow lark. He is very similar to our own that you would say at first sight, "Here is an old friend," but tho you might mistake him for a transplanted easterner you would very soon be convinced that he had imbibed the very spirit of the great free open praire for he is fairly bursting with song, a round full rollicking song that a friend in Dakota has translated "How's your equi 'lib' ri 'um '?" as much as to say that his is all right and wishing you the same.

Western Meadowlark

Western Meadowlark

Sturnella magna neglecta

Meadow beauty, meadow fern, meadowsweet.
Sweet words, sweet verse, meadow-verse.
An open, expansive verse. A grassy verse—pungent, warm, and prickly,
and, oh, so yellow.

The Meadowlark. I prefer all one word, Meadowlark.
Although my grandfather's two words, Meadow Lark, say yellow lark,
rainbow lark, glow lark.

A verse about to be mowed. Just mowed. Releasing its fragrance.
Do not mow while the Meadowlark nests in a domed cup of grass.

In 1844, Audubon discerned a difference between the Western and the Eastern
Meadowlark, and he named the Western *neglecta*.

More yellow running into the cheek.
And its voice: *a round full rollicking sound*.

Sixty-five years after Audubon noticed the Western Meadowlark's yellow cheek,
my grandfather shot three Meadowlarks flying over a low hill in a stubble field
among weed stalks.

My grandfather loved Meadowlarks for they were *fairly bursting with song*.

Field Notes
June 22, 1909

39. Dakota Song Sparrow
Fish Lake, N. D.
Nest set on bank of ditch under and back of overhanging
dead grass. Ditch small with running water between
two small lakes. Surroundings, open meadow with
bushes on hills nearby. Nest made of round grass-stems
with a lining of horse hair the same as the Eastern song
sparrow.

When bird was first flushed she crawled out of the nest
and off through the grass. The next time I came up in
back, and then she jumped down in the ditch and even
into the water. This time however she flew to the bushes
and afterwards both male & female were in plain sight
for some time. Birds same as light colored specimens
taken on praire.

Dakota Song Sparrow

Dakota Song Sparrow

Peterson, 1939: *Melospiza melodia juddi*

You know it's a club when the leader says
House Sparrow is a bird everybody is familiar with,
and gives you only a black-and-white drawing, albeit delicate,
of a male and female House Sparrow, he in front partially
obscuring her: *Passer domesticus domesticus.*

She soft-looking like heather, he rather fierce, like a little robber
outfitted with a jaunty black eye-mask and neckerchief.

Whereas the distinguishing mark of a Dakota, Robert discovered,
was an ink blot on its breast, a *messy* one at that.

Why messy? Why dingy? I think of her as pearl, as moon, as
a coalescence of cloud, as an opaline egg-like gem.

When does the Dakota Song Sparrow disappear from natural history
and become the Song Sparrow?
For at least forty years, Robert thought of his Dakota Sparrow.

So many sparrows!
Pine-woods, Lark, Seaside, Dusky Seaside, Grasshopper,
Dickcissel, which is about the size and build of a House Sparrow
(with which we are all familiar) with a fondness for alfalfa fields.

Northern Seaside Sparrow: *In parts of Florida, it is folly to attempt discrimination without collecting.*

Robert doesn't list Dickcissel, but he does Baird's, Tree, Savannah, White-crowned, Vesper, Lincoln, Chipping, Swamp, White-throated, Harris, English (or House), and Clay-colored.

With sparrows, I advance only as far as this:
often secretive, often brownish and streaked, with short conical bills, and the voice of *Melospiza melodia*: *sweet, sweet, sweet.*

Field Notes
June 23, 1909

41.   Least Flycatcher.
Nest saddled between side limb and main trunk 3
ft from ground on small poplar in bushy woodland.
Made of gray inner bark strips lined with white
vegetable wool and a few very fine grasses. All very
neat and smooth.

Saw the bird on nest and approached within 2
ft when she flew and did not return. There is a
possibility that it might be a Traill's. 4 eggs. cream
color. nearly complete inc.

Least Flycatcher

Peterson, 1939: *Empidonax minimus*

Being olive-gray, having white eye rings,
and white wing bars, being small,
like most Flycatchers,
the Least cannot easily be identified,
which is why Robert was unsure,
the Traill's being very like the Least.

The fact that the nest was saddled between side limb and main trunk,
the fact that the nest was three feet off the ground,
the fact that there were four cream-colored eggs (not speckled)
indicates a Least.
To complicate matters, since Robert's time,
the Traill's has been recognized as two species,

the Alder and the Willow.
The idea is to identify the tree in which the Flycatcher is perched,
alder or willow,
and if not alder or willow,
if it's a beech, say, or a poplar,
then the Flycatcher is a Least, the grayest of them all.

Summary of visit

I spent whole days pacing off certain sections of
pasture where the Baird's Sparrows were abundant
but was not successful until after the young had
hatched, when I located two nests. I came to have a
great deal of respect and admiration for this little bit
of bird life for he was seldom worried by my presence,
going calmly about his business now and then
stopping to trill a sweet little song from a weed stem,
in full confidence that his nest was too well hidden to
be found out by mortal eyes.

Song Drawings

Did you know that bird songs can be drawn?
With dashes, curves, and squiggles
spaces in between
kind of like a poem—a song poem.

Chickadee:

―――

― ――

White-throated Song Sparrow:

―――

―――

――― ――― ―――

Robert, did you hear the Least Flycatcher sing?

In your copy of *Field Guide to the Birds*, the one you signed "R.S. Judd,"
in 1947, when you were sixty years old,
a black and white picture compares "The Small Flycatchers:"

their songs
their habitats
their overall oliveness.

This is the Least Flycatcher's song
(grayest of the group):

—— or ——

set within farm, orchard, and woods.

This is the Alder Flycatcher's song
(brownest of the group):

set within swamp, thicket, and water.

The songs of the Flycatchers are not learned; the birds are born knowing them.

Field Notes
July 9, 1909

Had to drive to town and back in forenoon. After dinner went to look up a burrowing owl which E. T. had seen. Saw one of them sitting on a gopher mound on a gravel hill but could not get close enough for a shot. Found the hole where they were evidently nesting. It was an old gopher hole in the grass on the side of a knoll of sand at edge of grain field. There were several feathers, down, droppings, and a ball of little shells about the entrance so I take it to be inhabited.

Burrowing Owl

Burrowing Owl

Peterson, 1939: *Speotyto cunicularia*

I want to understand the moon,
how yesterday, in the morning, I saw its egg-white bulge
in the eastern sky, clouds drifting along, obscuring it,

then revealing it, as if it bloomed every few seconds,
rolled downstage, pirouetted. How my grandmother
loved owls. Did she know my grandfather hunted

Burrowing Owls in Cando, North Dakota, when he
was twenty-two? Six years before she married him.
Did she love owls before or after?

We used to give her owl-things—a scarf, a saltshaker.
My grandfather recorded his collections of eggs and birds.
The Burrowing Owl. Comical bird—its long legs (for an owl),

its bobbing and bouncing when agitated, its diving into a hole,
the gopher's hole it found; why not? It's quite capable (for an owl),
its rule-of-thumb. Funny bird. Its chattering, chuckling, cackling,

but liquid, tremulous. At night, its mournful *coo-co-roo*, its secret.
How yellow its eyes, how white its arched eyebrows, as if kabuki
queen, as if skeptical. Scowl-bird. Barrow, pillow, burr-bird.

My grandfather never noted the moon, only eggs, only nests,
only how many birds he shot. I wonder if my grandmother pulled
on her boots, went out into the night to look for owls.

Field Notes
July 16, 1909

It is a pretty sight to see the large flocks of Yellowlegs maneuvering, all keeping close together and whirling and darting at great speed.

Yellowlegs

An Alphabet of Yellowlegs

Air pockets in bones and feathers. Air inside and out.
You look like a Bun or a Bow, and you Bow.
Sometimes, especially from the back, you look like a Cello or a pear.
Remember those paper Doilies, lacy at the edges, and intricately cut?
Funny leg-Elbows! Actually, those are knees.
Such a pretty sight, your Flock, meaning cloud or a tuft of wool,
flashing Gold in the sun,
or a Halo, the kind that is Hammered or translucent.
You Illumine and are an Illumination, a subject and a verb.
Not all Jewels sparkle; some do.
A Knoll. What passes for a hill around here.
You love Lakes, small Lake animals, Lake mud.
Are you as yellow as the Moon? As silver or white?
Your Nest as round as.
Odd, this shimmering Opal.
I already said your crowd makes a Pretty sight, like a million Petals
or Pearls. Quill-bill. Quill-legs.
You are as yellow as my Rambling Roses, back home,
as the Sun. As brown as Sand.
Tweed, your whites and Tans mixed, little flocks.
Umbrella-legs, spokes-of-a-wheel-legs. Skinny bicycle.
I sat down to pick yellow Violets.
Darting and Whirling, keeping close together.
Are all birds eXtroverts, or just you?
Yellow violets, not purple or blue or white.
Zest. You are full of Zest, you ZigZag bird.

Summary of visit

One can not be long on the prairie without falling in love with the beautiful Franklin's Gulls. Can you imagine anything more pleasing or that would be more apt to relieve the monotony of a days plowing in a field where twice around is a days work, than a flock of these rosy pink, gray and black beauties circling low over the black freshly turned earth, or follow close in the furrow picking up the worms and insects.

Franklin's Gull

Larus pipixcan

What were they, all those gulls on Great Island last August
when the heat made the pastor's forehead glisten, and we
in our long pants, long-sleeved shirts, broad-brimmed hats,
like feathered gulls ourselves, not knowing what to look for—
gulls' white heads, yellow bills, their breasts' pale rosy bloom.

Cawing, pecking, swooping in their great congregations,
their rush of wings, along the sweep and roar of the surf,
the untramelled sand, what did we see on its floor, in its eddies
of curving lines, its beach clutter, its drifts of seaweed, horseshoe
crabs, in its shells? We only knew the great extent of the beach,

seals poking their ink-heads out of the sea to look at us, at each
other, flapping their slinky way in the swells. We swam in the bay,
changing into our suits behind a towel we held up for each other,
not that the boaters and sunbathers cared to look at us, to notice
our wrinkled northern bodies. Our warm, gritty sandwiches.

Who knows if they were Franklin's Gulls? More likely Laughing
Gulls, the smallest of gulls, which are hard to tell from Franklin's,
except, overhead, Franklin's white wing bars look like windows
transmitting light. We didn't know to look up, and we didn't know
Franklin's Gulls are of the Great Plains, their laugh high pitched.

Letter to Pop
August 15, 1909

Carrots are a very useful vegetable out here, they make good pie, and fine sweet pickles as good as pears; have mother try some.

Carrots as a Useful Vegetable

C as in carrot, cart, cook, or cough.
A as in have. Seemingly gentle, seemingly maybe. Aunt.
R as in pear and star. A barrel of carrots. A barrow.
R as in *le roi carotte* or *la reine*. Rabbit. As in request.
O as in Mother, as in orange, as in some. As in Pop.
T as in today, tomorrow, tear. As in try.
S as in suggest, sorrow, and son. Susie.

U as in upsetting or us. As the u in *your son*.
S as in some pickles or some pies. Send and sad.
E as in the end of prairie, please, or home.
F as in furrow or flower. Feathery. Fair.
U as in until, or understand, or utter.
L as in *it will be almost like leaving home*. As in lose and love. All.

Letter to Pop
August 15, 1909

We get out at a little after five in the morning, feed
and harness before breakfast and get into the field
before seven. Then we take an hour and half at noon
and work the teams until seven. It is nine by the
time we are ready for bed.

Growing Up Together

Robert was born in 1887.
 So was Marianne Moore.
Can you imagine?
 Bryn Mawr vs. a farm in Cando, North Dakota.

Mrs. Moore in the background staring at Marianne,
 mother vs. daughter.
Mother, Pop, Robert.
 Pop's letter seemed to have kind of a lonesome streak.

Reading at night by the basement window, by the light
 on the prairie. "So this
reading will be like
 living, then . . ." Mrs. Moore keeping house, as did Susie.

Right here I might as well tell what these terms signify:
 pothole, slough, coulee. I
feel lonesome myself
 sometimes, my mother, my love to yourself and the rest.

I don't think he ever felt intimidated, out
 of his element. I
don't think she ever
 did either, so they have that in common. Marianne

would have taken to the prairie. "Courting males in spring
   make a hollow three-syllabled
'booming' *oo-loo-woo*,
   suggesting the sound made by blowing across the

opening of a Coca-Cola bottle." Shooting
   birds? You could count feathers,
stripes, and spots. Name their
   colors, too, measure their wings, and collect quotations.

Even now, late as it is, the chickens are very
  poorly feathered and re-
quire careful handling
  to make a good specimen. "One hundred, fifty-word

description." You could make the birds into something else—
   or something else into
birds. "It is just as
if the flower were gradually turning into the bird."

From little words, wren, to big words, phalarope, "Words should
   be looked through, should be windows."
I wish someone would
  write. Goodbye for now my own dear mother and father.

Letter to Mother
August 29, 1909

*The boys commence school on Wednesday of this week
with the usual "Wish I didn't have to." They have
been having a great time at the farm, into everything
from circus riding to climbing the windmill tower.
What one does the others have to do after and a little
extra if possible.*

Percy and Rea

Percy T. Judd   (1899–1982)
Rea Davis Judd   (1901–1999)

Under the light of a fringed lamp, or by the light of a prairie window,
Percy studies in the library of North Dakota Agricultural College,
bent over his book and paper, writing, not noticing the young woman
across the way or the other men nearby, all posing, maybe, for folks
at home—look how we study!

Had he met Rea yet, or that other girl, the one Rea dumped a pail of water
on when she and Percy came back late, lingering at the bottom of the spiral
staircase? *I did not like her.* The time Percy tried to feed Rea cod liver oil,
and she vowed to marry him out of spite. *No, I loved him.* Percy was not
a good letter writer, always late

to school in the fall because of farm work: *I had decided never never to see
him again.* But when he showed up at the football game, she could not resist.
Senior year, life would be unbearable without him. Ah, they worked, he
in the animal heat of the barns, she in the hum of the home ec department.
And not to waste her education,

she taught two years in Grafton. When Percy said, we're through unless you
marry me now, she did, a bouquet of roses held close to tiny tucks in her bodice,
a single rose pinned to his thick wool lapel, their clear, open, hopeful faces.
Such beauty. They moved to the farm, Goodwater Farm, good air, good land,
goodness, and had that bunch of kids,

Phyllis being the last, and therefore the one who traipsed after Rea as she traveled the region teaching school, until she asked, at twelve, to be allowed to stay home, attend school in Cando and take care of the house and her father. Which she did, learning what Elmer and Susie learned, what Percy and Rea learned, that love of a prairie knoll carries the day.

Letter to Pop
Sept. 12, 1909

Still I believe I would rather shoot one old partridge
than a half dozen chickens. At this time of year
they are moulting and look like an old hen, all pin
feathers and ragged, and are about as unsatisfactory
game to carry home as anything I have ever seen. I
hope to get a few for specimens later when they are
fully feathered.

Molt

Dear girl, you said, molt is shed, lose, and drop.
Drip-drop like a gold tear, a hot coal, or a spit seed.

Your love is like that: rare and hard, wind and fold.
Molt: come, bone; come, coat; come, tail: sprout.

Life is a bulb, you said, under snow.
Life is a nest, you said, made over.

Your hands talk like a page.
Your ears play like words.

Molt is men of the long name who said what molt is,
who made molt rift, who bury molt away from hope.

Molt is only a room, where lawn.
Molt is only a pool, where leaf.

Your face is a flag, I feel like wave.
Your eyes are moss, I feel like seep.

My heart a barn of hens: molt, molt, a coop.
In spite of loss: her beak, her cheek, her feet.

Molt is spool, wind, and knit.
Molt is fret, thumb, and tune.

Love like dust.
Dust like a Bluebell.

Today sets the brow of agog
against the knee of give.

Field Notes

September 13, 1909
Saw a fine Long-billed Marsh-wren in the reeds.
Was singing within five ft of me.

September 30
Shot a Long-billed Marsh-Wren.

Marsh Wren

Long-billed Marsh Wren

Odd, aren't they, common names of birds?

You suppose the Long-billed Marsh Wren and the Short-billed Marsh Wren
are distinguished by the length of their bills.

But no one says anything about their bills, only where they live,
the Long-billed preferring cattails and the Short-billed preferring grasses.

How do they know, these wrens, these tiny birds flitting among the sticks,
which is which, cattails or grasses? Cattails, perhaps, being sturdier, taller,
more fragrant.

The Long-billed looks like a cattail, I'm beginning to think, a velvety brown
cylindrical thing, waving in the breeze of the marsh.

Maybe the Short-billed finds comforting soft grasses that whisper.

Tules, they also frequent tules, which are bulrushes, which are reeds.

Things even out; Sibley names the Long-billed and the Short-billed one bird,
the Marsh Wren.

Even though the Short-billed lacks the white eye stripe of the Long-billed,
and is smaller.

Ah, at least the Marsh Wrens are not House Wrens, which do not prefer grasses,
but gardens and towns, often nesting in odd places such as flowerpots, mailboxes,
and pockets of coats on clotheslines, which are like cattails if made of brown wool.

Field Notes
Oct. 23, 1909

The past week has been cold and cloudy with the exception of one day.

Have been hunting most of the time but with little success.

On the 15th was out all day. In the forenoon saw several large flocks of chickens but had no dog and did not succeed in killing one. Late in the afternoon succeeded in killing a fine Sharp-tailed Grouse. I flushed it from a patch of tall weeds where it had been all the afternoon as Elmer saw it there at noon.

A Fine Sharp-tailed Grouse

Pediocaetes phasianellus

Walking in the fields today, dogless, a shining cold,
this windy, winding, endless prairie,

I hunt; which patch of weeds are you hiding in,
thinking you are safe,
as quiet as a stone?

Little Pheasant of the Ground, spotted beauty,
harbored in your thicket, in your soundless mound of bronze,
which grass of molten gold?

Stuffed pillow-pouch,
speckled-copper feather-gown, all zipped-up and smocked,
bits of blue, flecks of light, meadow-glint and graze.

Up, you burst!
Smack, flap, and rush,
clatter and clack!
Kek,kek, kek, kek,
you shriek,
brown and copper and pale.

Tawny towel, shiny plow,
found, tossed, and rowed,
thrown, cracked, and felled.

You of the sharp tail, obvious when you fly,
you of the flash-grass hide-out,
you are stilled, you are fine, you are mine.

Field Notes
November 2, 1909

It is a great sight to see the white geese come in in regular order and drop like a handful of fluttering papers to the lake. They are always talking and it seems as though I could almost understand them.

My Grandfather

My grandfather is and is not of the hunters.

He speaks of them—the hunters—as if he himself is not a hunter.
But of course he goes out with Elmer at 6:30 a.m. to take down a goose.

He finds a goose with a broken wing.
When he holds it in his hands, he feels its heart beating.

And he hears the geese talking like children;
my grandfather was a child himself not so long ago.

He almost understands them, the goose words, the goose language.
Like townsfolk on a picnic. Sharing picnic food.

He observes their flying, their heading north,
their going out, their coming in,
their regular routine only interrupted by the hunters.

As if he is one of the geese, riding high up in the sunshine,
lazily floating along in a constantly changing formation.

The hunters violating the way of the geese.
With their continuous bombardment, shooting at the geese,
at my grandfather.

If it weren't for the hunters, my grandfather would be one
with the geese, and taking a goose, killing it, would be like killing him.

Skins
Nov. 2, 1909

240. Green-winged Teal
Nettion carolinensis (eye very dark brown)
Le. 15.15 Ex. 24.50
Was flying over praire going to lake.

Green-winged Teal

Green-winged Teal
Nettion carolinensis

1.

When you are the smallest dabbling duck possible, you wheel in the air
in large flocks, calling your crick-like whistle, thinking you are wild, but
in the blue spaces between the clouds, you are caught by a hunter who
isn't faster than you are, who is clumsy, but who was given a gun as a boy,

2.

and thinks it's natural to take you down, then remark on your beauty as he
would remark on a sunset, the ones in North Dakota, the ones that fill the
whole sky with a sudden vast light, before dark reaches up out of the prairie
with its clenched fist.

3.

In August of 1912, when you are twenty-five, on the cusp of marrying Edith,
you give your Green-winged Teal to Dr. Bishop, who builds a structure in his
backyard to house his specimens, the ones he's collected and the ones he's
accepted from you and other hunters like you.

4.

Its very dark brown eye, which you wouldn't observe unless you shot it; its
iridescent green head, which no human was supposed to touch, just gaze at
from far below, as if touching would wound the bird, would bruise it, would
nullify its magic. The white band in front of the wing: particular magic.

5.

Preferring mud flats, preferring the seeds and stems of aquatic vegetation:
bulrushes, pond-weeds, spike-rushes, and widgeon-grass. Also buttonbush.
When the hunter notes the white underbelly of the small flying duck, as
distinguished from a dark underbelly, he knows it's a Green-wing, and aims.

RESIDENT LICENSE
No. 149

Robert Judd Hunting License, Towner County, ND

Feathers Drop Out of Your Notebook

You tucked two feathers inside your field notebook.
My mother found them. I found them.

Only three people have touched these tiny feathers,
these silver-brown downy fluffs, in over one hundred years.

The feathers look as fresh as the day you pressed them here,
along with your Towner County hunting license,

and a pencil sketch of the underside of a bird,
an arrow pointing to a scratched-in dot, labeled "leg here."

How to describe the feathers?
They look like winter, or a prairie—

gray grass, gray rocks, gray sky.
A velvety gray, with a touch of cinnamon,

or chestnut. An animal gray. Almost like fur.
Untouchable, irresistible, breath.

Each time I open the notebook, the feathers try to escape,
to catch a current, to float in the dusty air.

Works Cited

Unless otherwise noted, the genus/species names of birds are the ones Robert Judd used in 1909. The following guides provided other species names. Some of the poems draw on the language of these guides.

Bull, John and John Farrand, Jr. *National Audubon Society Field Guide to North American Birds. Eastern Region*. Revised Edition, New York, Knopf, 1994.

Peterson, Roger Tory. *A Field Guide to the Birds*. Revised and Enlarged. Boston: Houghton Mifflin Company, 1939.

_____. *A Field Guide to the Birds.* Second Revised and Enlarged Edition. Boston: Houghton Mifflin, 1947.

Sibley, David Allen. *Sibley's Birding Basics*. New York, Knopf, 2002.
_____. *The Sibley Guide to Birds*. Second Edition. New York, Knopf, 2014.

***

The excerpts that preface each poem are from three notebooks that my grandfather kept during his stay in North Dakota; from a "Summary" he wrote after the visit, but which includes quotations from notes that haven't survived; and from letters he wrote to his parents and grandfather. The notebooks include two "field notes" and one "skins."

***

"Bobolink":

Emily Dickinson wrote this poem in 1859 when she was twenty-nine, just seven years older than Robert was when he observed and collected his Bobolink fifty years later:

"#54"

"Lethe" in my flower,
 of which they who drink,
 in the fadeless Orchards
 hear the bobolink!

Merely flake or petal
As the Eye beholds
Jupiter! my father!
I perceive the rose!

***

"Growing Up Together":

line 8: Robert's letter to Mother, August 8, 1909
lines 10–12, 32–33, 37–38: Owen S. Rogal, directions to students on reading.
lines 13–16: Robert's letter to Pop, April 19, 1909
lines 21–25: Peterson, 1939, p. 76
lines 29–32: Robert's Field Notes, October 23, 1909
lines 35–36: John Ruskin, "Love's Meinie," *The Complete Works of John Ruskin*, New York:
National Library Association, vol. XV, p. 65 [not dated]
lines 39–40: Robert's letter to Mother, July 5, 1909

***

"Feathers Fall Out of Your Notebook":

Robert's original hunting license was tucked inside one of his notebooks.

Acknowledgments

"Burrowing Owl" and "Western Meadowlark" (in slightly different versions), *Writing Workshop* Chapbook, vol. 1, Ruth Stone Foundation, 2019

"My Grandfather" (in a slightly different version), *Zig Zag Lit Mag*, Issue 7, Fall 2019

About the Author

Margaret Rogal grew up in Connecticut, not far from where her grandfather Robert Silliman Judd—the subject of these poems—was born and raised, and where he lived his entire life. Although a New Englander by birth and nature, Rogal spent thirty years in Iowa and Illinois, raising two daughters and working as a librarian. A graduate of Colgate University, Rogal studied poetry at the Iowa Summer Writing Festival, Augustana College, and the Bread Loaf Writers' Conference. Now a resident of Vermont, Rogal was a finalist for the Poetry of the Plains & Prairies Award and the Sundog Poetry Book Award. Her poetry has appeared in such journals as *Common Ground Review*, *Broad Street*, *Zig Zag Lit Mag*, *Miramar*, and *SALT*. *Field Notes* is her first book-length collection.

Photo courtesy of
Louise Cabot

About the Series

With some frequency, North Dakota State University Press receives manuscripts that are not quite book-length but still significant studies or literary works. In the past, we've sadly turned them away. Our new series, A Little Book about North Dakota, provides the opportunity to bring such works to the public.

Several years ago, when the press's editor in chief, Suzzanne Kelley, was conducting historical research in New Zealand, she spied the BWB Texts Collection, little books on a variety of New Zealand topics produced by Bridget Williams Books and prominently displayed in nearly every bookstore. Now, with dozens of "short books on big subjects," the BWB Texts are affordable, easy to carry while traveling, and chock full of interesting content of interest to New Zealanders. Each book measures only a few inches wide and tall and generally has somewhere between eighty and two hundred pages.

Enamored with the idea of the little book, Suzzanne posed the notion to her Certificate in Publishing students. One of the graduate students, Ana Rusness-Petersen also liked the idea. Ana set out to learn everything she could about little books as her publishing research project. Her findings include aspects of contemporary trends in format, content, production, marketing, and distribution, which NDSU Press has ably adopted for this new series.

In March 2020, Suzzanne set the idea before the members of the press's Editorial Board, where it was met with much enthusiasm. Suzzanne suggested Mike Jacobs—retired editor and publisher of the *Grand Forks Herald*—might serve as series editor, and the board members approved unanimously. When Mike accepted the invitation, the project began in earnest. Our series logo and cover designs are by award-winning graphic designer Jamie Trosen. Deb Tanner, also an award-winning designer and a long-time designer for NDSU Press, takes care of every aspect—aesthetic and technical—of the interior design.

Each Little Book about North Dakota measures 6" x 6" and contains a substantive and/or literary treatment of the history, science, social science, health, politics, literature, culture, or contemporary life in North Dakota. The possibilities for content are limitless, bound only by their connection to North Dakota.

Submissions of such works, which will undergo our blind peer review process for acquisition, may be sent to our online submissions portal at https://ndsupress.submittable.com/submit.

About the Press

North Dakota State University Press (NDSU Press) exists to stimulate and coordinate interdisciplinary regional scholarship. These regions include the Red River Valley, the state of North Dakota, the plains of North America (comprising both the Great Plains of the United States and the prairies of Canada), and comparable regions of other continents. We publish peer reviewed regional scholarship shaped by national and international events and comparative studies.

Neither topic nor discipline limits the scope of NDSU Press publications. We consider manuscripts in any field of learning. We define our scope, however, by a regional focus in accord with the press's mission. Generally, works published by NDSU Press address regional life directly, as the subject of study. Such works contribute to scholarly knowledge of region (that is, discovery of new knowledge) or to public consciousness of region (that is, dissemination of information or interpretation of regional experience). Where regions abroad are treated, either for comparison or because of ties to those North American regions of primary concern to the press, the linkages are made plain. For nearly three-quarters of a century, NDSU Press has published substantial trade books, but the line of publications is not limited to that genre. We also publish textbooks (at any level), reference books, anthologies, reprints, papers, proceedings, and monographs. The press also considers works of poetry or fiction, provided they are established regional classics or they promise to assume landmark or reference status for the region. We select biographical or autobiographical works carefully for their prospective contribution to regional knowledge and culture. All publications, in whatever genre, are of such quality and substance as to embellish the imprint of NDSU Press.

Our name changed to North Dakota State University Press in January 2016. Prior to that, and since 1950, we published as the North Dakota Institute for Regional Studies Press. We continue to operate under the umbrella of the North Dakota Institute for Regional Studies, located at North Dakota State University.